The Fight for Freedom

1750–1783

Morrill Middle School
Berryessa Union SD

Saddleback's *Graphic American History*

SADDLEBACK
EDUCATIONAL PUBLISHING
www.sdlback.com

ISBN-13: 978-1-59905-357-8
ISBN-10: 1-59905-357-8
eBook: 978-1-60291-685-2

Printed in Guangzhou, China
NOR/0913/CA21301739

17 16 15 14 13   5 6 7 8 9 10

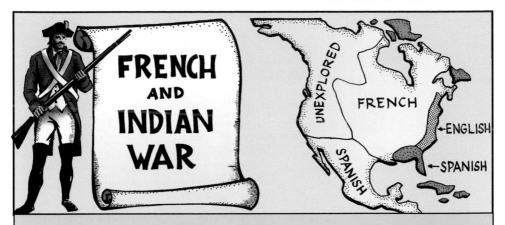

FRENCH
AND
INDIAN
WAR

By 1750, the English colonies occupied only a very small strip along the Atlantic coast. Population in the English colonies was increasing. Conflict between the English and French became certain because English settlers were pushing westward into French territory.

Young George Washington was a Virginia surveyor. He was asked to carry a letter through the wilderness to the French commander in the Ohio territory. It directed the French to leave land claimed by British forces. This was a dangerous journey in winter through country best known for Native Americans, bears, and rattlers.

They had a long, hard journey to the French headquarters.

From Governor Dinwinddie, of Virginia, sir.

The trip back to Virginia was even worse.

The French sent word back by Washington that they would remain. Again Washington was sent, this time with a force of men to build a fort on the river. They were attacked and forced back by the French.

England then sent General Edward Braddock with troops to defeat the French. George Washington was one of Braddock's aides.

Braddock was not familiar with wilderness fighting. Instead of relying on pack horses, he insisted on a great wagon train. Benjamin Franklin of Philadelphia helped him to acquire supplies.

He appealed to the Pennsylvania farmers.

If you don't hire out your wagons, the British Hussars may take them by force! Better to take the money.

Mr. Franklin, this is almost the only instance of ability and honesty I've known in these provinces!

Pennsylvania was the only colony to meet its quota for the great Conestoga wagons.

The problem: moving an army of 1,400 men and equipment from the Potomac River to the forks of the Ohio. Many axmen went ahead to cut trees and clear a rough road.

The foot soldiers advanced as British troops always advanced, in neat solid rows. Their bright red coats were brilliant in the sun.

Washington protested. This was not the way to fight the French.

We must fight them in open ranks, man to man.

The savages may be formidable to your raw American militia. On the King's disciplined troops, they will make no impression.

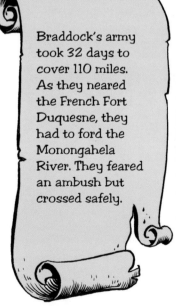

Braddock's army took 32 days to cover 110 miles. As they neared the French Fort Duquesne, they had to ford the Monongahela River. They feared an ambush but crossed safely.

All across safely, sir!

Good! We'll rush the fort.

Suddenly from the rear there was the sound of firing.

What's that?

Shots! And Indian war whoops.

One thousand Native Americans joined the French troops. They attacked the British from the cover of ravines and woods. The British troops, fighting in the open, in close formation, made good targets.

More than half the British troops, including General Braddock, were killed. Many more were wounded. Washington became a hero. Under his command the remaining British troops were able to retreat and save themselves.

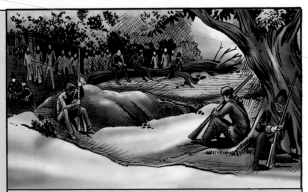

But Braddock's defeat made life harder for the British colonies. Both the Native Americans of the North and the French took advantage.

The English and French were at war over their possessions. England made a decision to conquer the French in the New World. She sent better troops and wiser officers to America. The colonies furnished more men and food. In 1759, the most important battle of the French and Indian War was fought at Quebec.

Quebec City was a natural fortress, on a high bluff above the St. Lawrence River. All routes leading to the city were guarded by General Montcalm's 14,000 French troops.

The English general, James Wolfe, moved British troops up the St. Lawrence River to Quebec.

Wolfe studied his maps and waited. He was expecting reinforcements by land.

Any word of General Amherst and his men?

No word, sir.

Wolfe thought out his problem. He quietly shifted his forces upriver. At last, after three months, he made his move.

With his army ready, General Wolfe was determined to surprise the French troops.

On the night of September 12, Wolfe and his army boarded a fleet of small boats. Quietly they floated downriver toward the city.

In a leading boat, Wolfe recited *Gray's Elegy Written in a Country Churchyard* to a young midshipman. Was he forecasting his own fate?

Suddenly from the shore a French sentry challenged them.

A French-speaking Scottish soldier answered. The French sentry decided the British were French, and gave no alarm.

* Who goes there?

The boats reached a little cove. Twenty-four volunteers tackled the rugged cliff route.

Taking the French guards by surprise, they overwhelmed them before they could make a sound.

The rest of the British troops swarmed up the 300-foot cliffs onto the grassy field at the top. At dawn the French looked out on an unbelievable sight: 4,500 British soldiers stood outside the city ready to fight.

Outside the city walls, as the French formed ranks and marched to meet the English, Montcalm warned his officers.

If it is necessary to fight them, it is necessary to crush them!

Now the French soldiers came running through the narrow streets of the city to meet the enemy.

Wolfe wanted an open-field battle, the kind he best knew how to fight. The French accepted his challenge and marched toward the British. Wolfe knew the power of accurate, concentrated firepower.

Three-fourths of his troops were stretched in a single line, which waited silently until the enemy was near. Then the command was given.

Fire!

Only two volleys were needed. The ground was covered with French dead and wounded.

Then the British charged, with Wolfe in the thick of the fighting. Suddenly he was struck by several bullets.

Support me! Don't let my brave soldiers see me fall. The day is ours.

So, the "Union Jack"* replaces the lilies of France!

Wolfe died knowing that he had won a great victory. Montcalm also was killed. The city of Quebec surrendered to the British.

*Flag of Great Britain

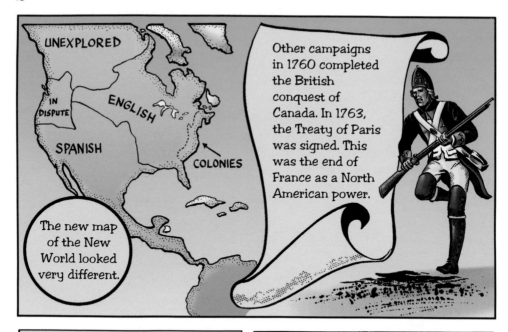

UNEXPLORED

IN DISPUTE

ENGLISH

SPANISH

COLONIES

The new map of the New World looked very different.

Other campaigns in 1760 completed the British conquest of Canada. In 1763, the Treaty of Paris was signed. This was the end of France as a North American power.

The name Yankee Doodle started, it was said, in Norwalk, Connecticut, when Colonel Thomas Fitch's regiment reported for duty. His sister thought the men looked shabby. She ran to the henhouse and returned with a handful of feathers.

Soldiers should have plumes! Here, stick a feather in your hat.

The men rode into New York state to join a British force. An English army surgeon saw them, laughed, sat down, and wrote a song. It made a hit with the redcoats.

*Yankee Doodle came to town upon a little pony. He stuck a feather in his hat and called it macaroni.**

At the end of the French and Indian War, the colonists were happy. They were proud to be part of the powerful British empire. They were thankful that the French threat had been removed from their frontier.

hey had found they could fight as well as the English soldiers—sometimes better.
t, to the redcoated British soldiers, any colonial militiaman was "Yankee Doodle."

* fancy decoration

Most colonies included land that extended inland over the Appalachian Mountains and into the Ohio territory. Hundreds of settlers had moved there, and more planned to go. The settlers felt that without the French to arm the Native Americans, they could protect themselves.

The Native Americans were angry after the French defeat. They feared losing too much of their land to the settlers. They organized and fought as never before.

In 1763, the great Ottawa chief, Pontiac, spoke to the Native Americans of many tribes. He persuaded them to attack all the English forts and settlements from Lake Superior to the Gulf of Mexico.

They wiped out isolated farmhouses.

Pontiac's success encouraged Miamis, Illinois, Weas, Kickapoos, Mascoutens, Delawares, and Shawnees to join the war for liberation.

There were many bitter battles before the British finally brought in enough men to stop them.

King George issued the Proclamation of 1763, forbidding the colonists to move into the territory west of the mountains. The English felt it would be easier to make peace with the tribes with no settlers to complicate matters.

In Boston, John Hancock was a wealthy merchant.

A tax on every legal document? Impossible!

Paul Revere was a silversmith.

A tax on every copy of a newspaper? No!

Sam Adams was a town official.

Only our assemblies can tax us—not the English!

The war had cost the English a lot of money. Now it had to keep a big army in the colonies to protect them. This was expensive. In 1765, the Stamp Act was passed requiring the colonists to pay a tax on all sorts of items.

Talk to your friends. Get them out to town meetings. Write to the papers. Make a speech!

These three men got together with others and held a meeting to make plans. They would oppose the tax!

A wave of protest swept through the colonies. Ministers preached against the new law. People gathered in the streets and in taverns everywhere. Groups called "Sons of Liberty" were formed.

On the day the tax law was to go into effect, there was trouble all over the country.

In New York, the Sons of Liberty burned the tax collector's coach.

In South Carolina, they captured the fort where the stamps were stored.

In Boston, a dummy figure of the collector was hanged from the Liberty Tree.

The stamp sellers quickly resigned their jobs. Many hid to save their lives.

Death to the man who offers a stamp to sell!

There he goes! After him!

No, no! I resigned!

Americans also refused to buy British-made goods.

George Washington recited to the Virginia Assembly a list of things he would not buy.

Many luxuries can be dispensed with: London shoes and clothing, for example.

In the cities, young women met to spin cloth and knit stockings.

We will call ourselves Daughters of Liberty and stop buying from England.

English merchants and manufacturers suffered from the boycott. They protested to the King. In 1766, the Stamp Act was repealed. Americans were very happy. In Boston, the Sons of Liberty met under the Liberty Tree to celebrate.

No one can tax Americans but Americans!

No taxation without our consent!

But the English did not agree. They had not given up the right to tax the colonies. In 1767, they passed new taxes on such things as paper, paint, glass, and tea. The tax was to be an import duty paid when the goods were brought into the country. Once again the Americans fought back.

Smuggling became patriotic.

So did weathered gray houses.

No, we won't paint the house this year!

British troops were to keep order and enforce collection of the taxes. Law officers were given warrants allowing them to search any home or building for smuggled goods.

Well, I never! Tracking up my clean floor and mussing my linens!

Pamphlets protesting these acts were printed and read throughout the colonies.

Benjamin Franklin of Philadelphia spoke in London to the British House of Commons.

I tell you, if troops are sent to the colonies to enforce obedience, they will not find a revolution there, but they may well create one!

Nevertheless, at the request of the Massachusetts governor, a war ship and two regiments of soldiers were sent to Boston in 1768. The people hated them. Crowds jeered and threw stones. Then came the night of March 5, 1770, and the Boston Massacre.

A crowd began threatening some of the soldiers.

Let's drive them out! They've no business here!

Lobster-back, bloody-back,* go home!

A soldier pushed one of the protesters into a snow bank.

Help! He's killing me!

*Nickname for British soldiers because of the red coats they wore.

More soldiers came to help. The crowd pressed closer. An African-American man, Crispus Attucks, ran forward and tried to seize a soldier's gun.

Come on! Don't be afraid! They daren't fire!

The soldiers opened fire. Crispus Attucks and four other men were killed. Nine British soldiers were later arrested on a charge of murder.

The next day a great crowd came to a meeting called by Sam Adams.

They are bloody butchers! Not another night should we allow them in Boston!

Adams and a committee went to the governor.

I tell you, sir, nothing can hold back the people if the soldiers remain in Boston!

The frightened governor sent the troops down the harbor to Castle William. The custom officers went with them.

The British reconsidered. All taxes were repealed except on tea. Even so, English tea was cheaper than smuggled tea. But, in paying the tea tax colonists would be agreeing to England's right to tax them. So, ships carrying tea were not allowed to unload. Then three ships arrived in Boston Harbor.

Church bells rang out, calling patriots to a meeting.

It's the tea!

The governor must be made to send it back to England!

But the governor would not send it back. A great meeting was held at Old South Meeting House. Some of the men were strangely dressed.

Boston Harbor a teapot tonight!

The Mohawks are coming!

In a house on Summer Street, Mrs. Brewer helped her husband and his friends darken their faces.

This burnt cork will do it!

In a blacksmith's shop, men darkened their faces with coal dust.

Led by Sam Adams, about 50 men disguised as Native Americans boarded the three ships.

They chopped open and threw into Boston Harbor chests of tea valued at $50,000.

No one will pay a tax on saltwater tea!

At that time, of course, there were no telephones, telegraph, radio, cars, railroads, or planes. Messages were carried by foot or on horseback. Communication between towns and between colonies was difficult and slow.

In 1772, Sam Adams proposed to the Boston town meeting that it set up a new committee.

We need committees in each town to write and send letters, keeping patriots aware of the latest news.

The Committees of Correspondence were a success. Thomas Jefferson in Virginia carried the idea farther.

We need such committees in all 13 colonies, to keep patriots in touch all over the country.

King George was angry and closed the Boston port. War ships were stationed to prevent ships from entering or leaving. The governor was to rule Massachusetts with no town meetings or elections to be held.

Troops were brought in to Boston again and quartered in the citizens' homes. If you had a spare room, you had redcoats living in it.

The Committee of Correspondence went into action. Paul Revere rode all the way to Philadelphia to carry the news of these Intolerable Acts.

Things are very bad in Boston!

The English thought these punishments would warn the other colonies to behave. They did not believe the other colonies would mind what happened to Massachusetts. They were wrong.

All over the colonies, flags flew at half-mast.

If it happens to Boston, it could happen to us!

Got some rice here from Georgia and Carolina, sir!

Wagonloads of food arrived from everywhere, so that Bostonians could eat in spite of the closed port.

Old Israel Putnam walked a hundred miles from Connecticut to bring a flock of sheep.

Wouldn't want you folks to go hungry!

Militiamen drilled on village greens in every town.

If England means to take away our liberties, we mean to defend them!

More and more, the patriots who were exchanging letters wanted to meet face to face and plan united action. Such a meeting took place in September 1774. Delegates from all the colonies except Georgia met in Philadelphia as the First Continental Congress.

Present were men whose names would go down in history. Many had never traveled before. They had a lot to talk about together.

John Adams (a cousin of Sam's) was surprised at the questions he was asked.

Why does Massachusetts hang Quakers, Mr. Adams?

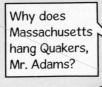

Why, we haven't hanged Quakers for a hundred years!

He was also surveying churches. He went every Sunday—to a different church.

Very interesting! I've never seen a Catholic church in Boston.

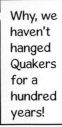

The Congress agreed to resist the Intolerable Acts and to remain united to protect their rights. They requested that King George do away with the unjust acts. They also agreed to stop trading with England until this was done.

Committees of Safety were set up in every town to plan for defense. On farms, men made their own gunpowder and bullets.

John Hancock headed the Massachusetts committee.

Sir, we'll be ready day or night, at a minute's notice!

The Massachusetts troops became known as Minutemen.

The King made General Gage governor of Massachusetts. With war ships in the harbor and troops quartered in the town, Gage controlled Boston. But there were 400,000 people in the state of Massachusetts!

The King does not understand the rebels are ready to revolt. They are storing arms and supplies.

In England, King George received an alarming report from Gage.

The New England governments are in a state of rebellion. Blows must decide whether they are subject to this country or independent.

It was up to General Gage to strike the blows. He decided on two steps. He would arrest those rebel leaders, Sam Adams and John Hancock, and ship them to England to be tried for treason. And he would seize the war supplies that the colonists were storing in Concord. He ordered his troops to move very secretly.

But Paul Revere had a committee watching every move of the British.

Seeing unusual activity, Revere arranged a signal with the sexton of the Old North Church.

I'll watch for lanterns in the belfry!

The night of April 18, 1775, was clear and cold. Across the river from Boston, Revere waited. Some 800 British troops marched out to their boats, and two little lights shone out from the church steeple.

The signal! The British troops are moving!

Be on your way!

Revere rode through the countryside, stopping at every farmhouse.

Spread the word! The British are coming!

Church bells sounded the alarm in the night.

A British patrol challenged Revere, but he spurred his horse away.

Halt! Or I'll fire!

Sam Adams and John Hancock were waiting in Lexington to leave for the second meeting of the Congress. Hancock wanted to stay and fight.

Mr. Hancock, your duty is to get to the Congress and win us their support!

John Brown... Jonas Parker... Sylvanus Wood...

Minutemen leaped from their beds and seized their guns. On Lexington Green, Captain John Parker called the roll.

In the early morning of April 19, 1775, Major Pitcairn rode into Lexington at the head of 800 British troops. He found a line of Minutemen facing him across the village green.

Someone fired a shot—then shots rang out from both sides. The war had begun. This battle lasted only eight minutes. The Americans withdrew, leaving eight dead and ten wounded. The British moved off toward Concord.

☆ ★ ☆ ★ ☆ ★ ☆

Meanwhile, in Concord, awakened at two o'clock in the morning by the alarm bells, the people had been busy.

The valuable supplies were loaded onto oxcarts.

Boys and girls hurried the oxen along toward hiding places in the woods.

Reaching Concord and finding little of value, the angry British set fire to the courthouse. Then they moved on to North Bridge to destroy it.

The Concord Minutemen were under the command of Major James Barrett.

Move the men to higher ground beyond the bridge.

The British approached the bridge from one side, the Minutemen from the other. The British opened fire. Major Buttrick called out to his Americans.

Fire, follow orders. For God's sake, fire!

The Americans fired. The British fell back.

The King's best soldiers were retreating from American farmers! Now the British retraced their march, while Minutemen fired at them from behind every tree and stone wall.

How can you fight an enemy you can't see?

When the unhappy British troops reached Boston at last, they had lost nearly 300 men.

In Boston they found themselves besieged. Farmers with their flintlocks came from New Hampshire, Connecticut, Rhode Island. In a few days an unorganized army of 16,000 Americans held General Gage and his men bottled up in Boston.

General Gage and his troops waited, cut off from the country outside, separated from England by 3,000 miles of sea. On May 25, a ship arrived bringing reinforcements and three major generals, Howe, Clinton, and Burgoyne.

The generals made plans.

From these low hills, they could bombard Boston. We must move first.

But the Americans had the same idea. On the night of June 16, rebel troops moved onto Breed and Bunker Hills.

We'll build breastworks* here. Dig, men!

Throughout the next morning, the Americans waited.

Remember, men, don't fire until you see the whites of their eyes!

At the quick-step, men!

Howe was ordered to dislodge the Americans. He led his troops in person, their bayonets gleaming in the sun.

* A temporary fortification

The British troops advanced.
The Americans waited. Then they fired.

Fire low, aim at the white waistbands and pick off the officers!

The American fire was deadly. The British troops went down in waves. Then they broke and ran.

The colonists received their support from many nationalities, and thousands of African Americans fought on the American side from Bunker Hill to the end of the war.

Twice the British advanced; twice they broke and ran. At last the American ammunition ran out, and on the third charge the British went over the breastworks.

★ ★ ★

In the Battle of Bunker Hill the British lost 1,054 men, the Americans 441. "Another such victory would have ruined us," said General Clinton. Most of all, it proved that Americans could throw back the best regular troops of Europe.

News of the siege of Boston spread rapidly. It reached Ethan Allen in Vermont.

Whoever holds Ticonderoga controls the route from Canada.

And that's the way the British could bring in reinforcements.

What the Americans need at Boston are cannons!

There are plenty of cannons at Fort Ticonderoga!

So Ethan Allen and his Green Mountain Boys set off through the woods for the British Fort Ticonderoga on Lake Champlain.

They approached the fort before daylight on May 10, overpowered the sleepy sentry, and pounded on the door of the commanding officer.

On the same night that Fort Ticonderoga was captured, patriot leaders were meeting in Philadelphia for the Second Continental Congress. There were urgent decisions to make. The country was up in arms.

In Philadelphia, as in other cities, militia paraded through the streets.

"Liberty or death." That is their motto!

The Congress made two important decisions. They adopted the colonial troops gathered around Boston as the Continental Army, and they appointed George Washington of Virginia as its commander in chief.

Washington took command at Cambridge on July 3.

Why don't we have a New England man?

That would make it too much a New England army. The whole country's in on this.

Washington was shocked at the conditions he found. He faced almost impossible problems.

We are without money in our treasury, powder in our magazines, or arms in our stores.

I'm going home to get my crop in, no matter what he says!

Why does he think he can order us around—just because he's an officer!

Sometimes it looked as if he would be without men. Americans did not like to take orders. That's why they were fighting the British. And they tended to go home when the need arose.

But Washington worked to build an army. And in January, General Knox arrived with the cannons from Ticonderoga.

One night in early March, an army with shovels moved on to Dorchester Heights.

We'll dig in here, men.

The next morning, Washington held a position from which Boston could be bombarded.

The British commander realized that he could no longer hold Boston. On March 17, he loaded his troops onto ships and sailed for Halifax. With him went 1,100 Boston Tories.*

But Washington knew the British would come back. He felt they would attack New York. He moved his army there.

He ordered the building of new forts on Manhattan Island.

Come, men! Who'll sign up to fight under General Washington?

Recruiting remained a serious problem. Officers went into the streets to try to enlist men.

*Americans who sided with the English king

At the same time important events were taking place at the Congress. Lee of Virginia introduced a resolution.

That these colonies are, and of right ought to be, free and independent states ...

... That they are absolved from all allegiance to the British Crown.

I second the motion!

Hear, hear!

Thomas Jefferson was elected to write the declaration. He shut himself up in his boardinghouse room.

We hold these truths to be self-evident that all men are created equal ...

The Declaration of Independence was accepted by Congress on July 4, 1776. John Hancock was the first to sign it.

I'll write my name large enough for King George to read without his spectacles!

John Adams wrote to his wife:

... it will be celebrated by succeeding generations as the great anniversary festival. It ought to be solemnized with pomp and parade, with shows, games, sports, guns, bells, bonfires ... from this time forward ...

And so the 13 colonies became the United States, and July 4th became Independence Day.

The announcement of the Declaration was greeted by cheers. Church bells rang, cannons fired. Washington had it read to the army.

New Yorkers, to celebrate, pulled down a statue of King George. Later the lead was used to make 40,000 bullets.

But soon the British fleet sailed into New York Harbor with a well-trained army of 30,000 men. To oppose them, Washington had less than half as many raw troops, poorly equipped and poorly fed. His only choice was to retreat, again and again, making each meeting as costly as possible for the British.

The British could have wiped out his entire army. Helped by heavy fog, Washington moved 9,000 men, along with equipment and provisions, across the East River to fight again.

Not everyone supported the war. When Washington's army was forced into New Jersey with the British hot on its heels, the New Jersey population did nothing to help.

Instead of turning out to defend their country, they are submitting as fast as they can!

Washington called their conduct "infamous."

They thought the British were winning, so they flocked to take an oath of loyalty to the king.

Imagine! Hiring Hessians to fight against fellow Englishmen!

King George had hired German troops from Hesse to fight for him. This made Americans very angry.

Now the Hessian troops, wintering in New Jersey, helped themselves to anything they wanted.

Here! You can't do that! I signed up with the king!

They looted stores and homes. They took away wagonloads of goods.

One soldier even managed to bring a grandfather clock back to New York on horseback!

This paper does no good. He can't read English!

From now on I'll stick with General Washington.

Washington's situation seemed hopeless. His army, now only 3,000 ragged, hungry, and cold men were pushed across the Delaware River into Pennsylvania. The British and many other people were sure that the Americans must give up. Congress fled from Baltimore to Philadelphia.

But Washington did not give up. Some 1,200 Hessians were stationed across the river in Trenton. He made a plan.

They make much of Christmas in Germany. The Hessians will drink a great deal of beer and have a dance.

On Christmas night we'll take cannons and 2,700 men across the river.

It was a terrible night, with sleet and snow. Many of the Americans had no shoes. The boats had to push their way through floating ice. Who would dream that an army could do it?

At eight the next morning, the Americans attacked. The Hessians were taken completely by surprise.

It was a great victory. Washington captured 900 prisoners and many arms. If gave new life to the American cause.

The British realized that the Americans were not about to surrender. They made new plans.

We will move up from New York and down from Canada, cutting off New England from the rest of the country!

A large army under General Burgoyne was to move to Albany, New York, from Canada. Like other British generals, Burgoyne knew little about traveling in America.

I'll need several trunks of uniforms and many cases of wine.

His officers had their own baggage, of course. And many of them brought wives and even children. They traveled very slowly through woods and swamps.

After leaving Lake Champlain they were under almost constant attack from New York and New England militiamen.

Running low on supplies, Burgoyne sent a force of Hessians to capture American supplies at Bennington, Vermont. Patriot John Stark recruited volunteers to resist the attack.

A messenger reached Concord during Sunday services and entered the church.

General Burgoyne is on the march. If we all turn out, we can cut him off.

My parishioners, if you are willing to go, you had better leave.

All the men in the meeting house rose and went out. This was typical of the New England response. Some 2,000 militiamen gathered at Bennington. General Stark made a prediction.

We'll beat them today, or tonight Molly Stark's a widow!

Stark and his men won a great battle over Burgoyne's soldiers.

Burgoyne was defeated again at Bemis Heights on the Hudson.

The fortifications were built by a young Polish engineer, Thaddeus Kosciusko, who had come to fight for freedom with the Americans.

Burgoyne never reached Albany. On October 17, 1777, he surrendered his entire army to General Gates at Saratoga.

The fortunes of war, General Gates, have made me your prisoner.

Burgoyne's defeat raised American morale, weakened British morale, and persuaded France to enter the war with the Americans. Benjamin Franklin had long been at the French Court working for this result.

Mr. Franklin, we have decided upon a treaty of alliance with your country.

Sire, America will be forever grateful.

Signed on February 6, 1778, this treaty provided that French men, money, and naval vessels would be used to help the Americans defeat England.

The young French Marquis de Lafayette had not waited for a treaty. He had already contributed both money and his services as an aide to Washington.

The cause of America is the cause of all mankind.

Baron Von Steuben, a German nobleman, also joined Washington's army.

He taught the raw troops discipline and drill.

But Washington would not know of the French treaty until May. Before that, at Valley Forge, he and his army had to live through the bitterest winter of the war.

First the men built huts for themselves.

A farmhouse is ready for your quarters, General.

No, no! I will stay in a hut until my men are housed.

The men had few blankets, ragged clothes, and worst of all, little food. Washington wrote Congress that the army must "starve, dissolve, or disperse" without more supplies.

What is your supper, lads?

What's for Thanksgiving dinner?

Firecake* and water, sir.

And for dinner!

And for breakfast!

A leg of nothing and no turnips!

*Soggy, tasteless bread mixture of flour and water cooked over open fire

42

My poor men, you can track them by their bloody footprints.

Only 20 miles away, in Philadelphia, General Howe and his officers lived in luxury.

A ball tonight? Good! Good!

Tories flocked to his parties. Even young patriot belles could not always resist the social scene.

I hope Peggy doesn't catch scarlet fever.*

*Falling in love with a British redcoat

More than 2,500 soldiers died at Valley Forge from illness and exposure. But somehow Washington held the army together. In May came news of the French treaty.

We will celebrate with a dress parade.

General, this will display the training you have given the troops.

Good!

The review of the troops went off smoothly. When 13 cannons fired as a signal, the whole army cheered.

Long live the king of France!

There was little the United States could do to challenge the war ships of the mighty British navy. But thousands of American seamen in smaller vessels, commissioned as privateers, harassed and captured British merchant ships. After the French treaty opened French ports to American ships, they made raids on the British coasts.

They left buildings and ships burning.

After one such raid, John Paul Jones, an American commander, challenged the British frigate *Serapis.*

What ship is that?

Come a little closer and I will tell you.

Jones' ship, the *Bonne Homme Richard,* opened fire. The *Serapis* fired back. The guns of the big, new *Serapis* soon crippled the American ship. Jones ordered his ship lashed to the *Serapis,* pirate-fashion.

There was fierce, close-quarter fighting. Then the British captain called to Jones.

Are you ready to surrender?

Sir, I have just begun to fight!

Three hours later the most famous sea battle of the war ended in an American victory!

George Rogers Clark of Kentucky had lived through many Native American raids. In 1778, he went to see the Virginia governor.

Sir, the British are giving the Indian tribes money and ammunition to attack American settlers.

If we capture the British forts between the Ohio River and the Great Lakes, we'll stop the Indian trouble.

A small band of rangers was outfitted. Clark led them into the Northwest Territory. They took the towns of Kaskaskia and Vincennes, Illinois, without a fight. The French-Canadian inhabitants had no love for the British. They took an oath of allegiance to the United States. Father Gibault, a French priest, was helpful.

The French king has come over to the American side.

The Indians like the French. We will tell them the French king is angry that they fight for the English.

But while Clark was at Kaskaskia, the British recaptured Vincennes.

We must march 180 miles quickly, before they can be reinforced.

They covered 180 miles in eight days, despite the raw February weather. But outside of Vincennes were five miles of flooded land.

It would take days to go around. We must go through it!

Men stumbled through the icy water protecting their guns.

Those who could no longer walk used canoes.

The Rangers surrounded the fort. Their sharpshooters were so deadly that the British could not man the cannonports and loopholes without being shot down. Soon the British surrendered.

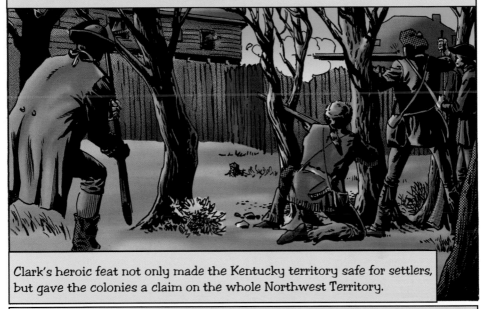

Clark's heroic feat not only made the Kentucky territory safe for settlers, but gave the colonies a claim on the whole Northwest Territory.

Also in 1778, General Clinton was made commander of the British forces. He moved the war to the South. Despite help from the French fleet, the Americans lost Savannah and all of Georgia.

Another Polish volunteer, Count Pulaski, led 200 cavalrymen into action at Savannah.

Bravely charging the enemy lines, Pulaski was shot down and killed.

In early 1779, Clinton sailed from New York for Charleston with 7,000 redcoats.

There is strong support for the king in the Carolinas. The Tories will help us.

Charleston fell to the British. The news reached Washington.

Charleston taken and 5,500 troops captured! This is our worst defeat of the war.

General Clinton, at Charleston, issued a harsh proclamation.

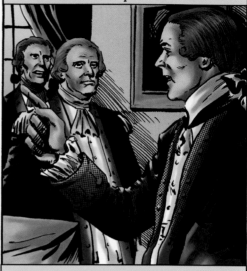

Tell the people that anyone helping the patriots will be hunted down and killed!

Patriot men, women, and children were homeless. Their houses were burned and their livestock slaughtered.

Washington had plans.

But Congress appointed General Gates. And Gates did everything wrong. In the battle of Camden, when his militia broke and ran, Gates turned his horse and galloped away.

If General Greene were in command in the South, I believe he could save us.

He galloped for 60 miles, right out of the war, disgracing himself and ending his army career.

It seemed that the British had won. Clinton returned to New York, leaving Cornwallis in charge. Cornwallis gave orders to Cal Ferguson.

Take 1,000 men into the mountains and enlist Tory troops.

Ferguson enlisted 1,200 Tories. He also stirred up the patriots.

If we get together, we can teach those Tories a lesson.

I've got 260 men.

I can raise 240.

These volunteers rode all night and caught up with Ferguson's men at King's Mountain. The British seemed in a strong position at the top of a slope.

They overlooked the fact that the slope was wooded, and the patriots were woodsmen and sharpshooters. Moving from tree to tree, the patriots surrounded them.

The victory at King's Mountain was a turning point. Now Congress put General Greene in charge of the Southern army.

We fight, get beat, rise, and fight again.

we're beat,
he British lose
do!

Cornwallis gave up in Carolina and moved his troops to Yorktown, Virginia. And in Connecticut, Washington met with the French general, Rochambeau.

I have word that the French fleet is sailing for Virginia.

If we move quickly enough, we can crush Cornwallis and destroy his army.

Your troops and my troops and those of General Lafayette will surround him on land—and de Grasse's fleet will bottle him up from the sea!

From Connecticut and New York the French and Americans quickly marched south. The plan worked perfectly. Cornwallis, surrounded and outnumbered, had only one hope.

I am sure General Clinton will send reinforcements!

But Washington had fooled Clinton into believing an attack would be made on New York, so Clinton kept his troops there.

The Allied forces dug in, moved their trenches closer, and brought in their heavy artillery to bombard Yorktown.

Colonel Alexander Hamilton led the attack on an important enemy position.

Push on, boys!

The fort's our town.

The same night a similar position was taken by French troops.

Who goes there?

Vive le roi!*

On October 17, 1781, a British drummer appeared on the wall. Beside him, an officer waved a white flag.

Look! A white flag! They're surrendering!

On October 19, General Washington, with Rochambeau beside him, rode out to receive the formal surrender.

As the British troops marched out to give up their arms, their band played a march called "The World Turned Upside Down."

* Long live the king

Cornwallis' sword was handed to the American General Lincoln.

Later, news of Cornwallis' defeat reached the king's chief minister in London.

Oh, God! It is all over!

The fighting was over. But it took more than a year to persuade the king that his "upstart colonies" had won.

Benjamin Franklin, John Adams, and John Jay represented the colonies at a peace conference in Paris. On February 3, 1783, a treaty was signed giving an independent United States of America all land south of Canada, east of the Mississippi, and north of Florida.

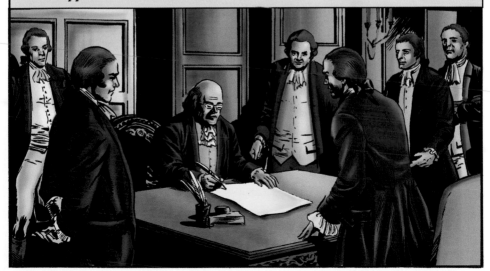

The British had held New York throughout the war. At last, on November 23, they sailed away and Washington marched in, leading his ragged army.

They are our troops! I love them all the more because they are so forlorn!

After eight long, hard years, George Washington was free to return to his family and his Virginia home. He said farewell to his officers.

With a heart full of love and gratitude, I take leave of you.

Perhaps the last words should be said by a typical revolutionary soldier, Joseph Plumb Martin.

Everyone has heard of the soldiers being tracked down by the blood of their feet on the frozen ground. The thousandth part of their sufferings has not, nor ever will be told.